The Co-Dependent Relationship

An Essential Guide to Overcoming Codependency and Eliminating Controlling Behavior from Your Relationship

by Josslyn King

Table of Contents

Introduction..1

Chapter 1: What Exactly Is Co-Dependent Behavior?
....9

Chapter 2: Realizing Where It Stems from 15

Chapter 3: Recognizing Childhood Trauma 19

Chapter 4: Gaining New Perspectives 25

Chapter 5: Understanding a Co-Dependent Partner
....33

Conclusion..37

Introduction

"It's late! What time is he coming home tonight?"

"Did he remember to pick up our son from football practice or did he wind up drinking in a bar again?"

"When will he ever learn to be more responsible? Doesn't he know that he's destroying our family?"

Jane's thoughts are killing her as she waits for her alcoholic husband, John. She spends the whole day pouring over her husband's alcoholism, how to fix it and how to make him the responsible husband and father that he ought to be.

Jane is a good wife and mother. She does her best to take care of her children and husband but she neglects herself. She has the tendency to overlook her own needs and feelings. Inside, she feels that she is being taken for granted and that no one cares about her. However, she also feels guilty for having those thoughts. She thinks that by asserting her needs and feelings, she is being selfish. She believes that if she were a good homemaker, she should be able to serve and love her husband in an unconditional way, despite his own flaws. What Jane fails to see is the reality of her situation. In reality, she is having a difficult time believing that her needs and feelings are also important. Instead of taking care of herself, she is trying to control John.

On the other side of town, Mark seeks help from a therapist. He tells his therapist about his family. *"I grew up in a happy family. Everything was pretty normal so I'm not really sure why I'm here. I'm not even sure if I need to be here. Nobody was abusive in our family and nothing traumatic happened during my childhood. All I know is that I feel so empty. It feels like something is missing in my life."* Mark continued saying that he is good with adjusting to other people. He explains that he can easily read people's personalities and conform to them. He admits that he is a people pleaser but at the same time, he is confused. He cannot figure out exactly what he needs, feels, or wants. Despite his friendly disposition, he feels empty and disconnected from his own self and other people. *"I feel like I'm some machine on auto pilot."*

Meanwhile outside of town, Peter is on vacation with his in-laws. His wife and kids are enjoying their holiday together as a family, and Peter is acting like he is enjoying it too. However, deep inside, he feels extremely unhappy. He doesn't want to go on a trip with his in-laws but he doesn't want to disappoint his wife. Even if he wants to do something different, he keeps quiet about it. He hides his feelings in general. This doesn't only happen when they are on vacation. This has become Peter's way of life. He often gets into fights with his wife because he feels like she is not sensitive to his needs. He refuses to face his own fears of being open about his thoughts and feelings. Instead, he takes it out on his wife who meanwhile has no idea why he is acting this way.

Jane, Mark, and Peter all have the same problem. The three of them are struggling with co-dependency. This phenomenon was initially studied by medical professionals in the marriages of alcoholics. Therapists and counselors working with individuals struggling with alcoholism noticed that they typically had spouses who were also facing psychological issues due to their partner's alcoholism. These spouses are often absorbed in trying to fix, rescue, or "save" their alcoholic partner but their efforts only tend to make the problem worse. Medical professionals refer to these spouses as "co-alcoholics." Later, they changed it to the more appropriate "co-dependent."

Co-dependents are individuals who are addicted, not to harmful substances, but to a destructive pattern of relating to the people around them. Jane fits in the classic description of a co-dependent because she displays rescuing behavior which further enables her husband's irresponsible lifestyle. Rather than putting up a limit on what she can tolerate, Jane keeps bailing him out of the consequences of his choices. For example, if John skips a day at work because of a hangover, Jane voluntarily lies for him by calling his boss and making up excuses. She also works overtime on her own job because John cannot provide enough for their family.

Even if Jane does not **like** saving her husband, on a deeper level she actually **wants** to do so. Taking on the role of a savior and a caretaker gives her a sense of identity, drives away her fear of loneliness, and maintains the illusion that if she loves him unconditionally, John will eventually come to his senses. Apparently for Jane, the thought of giving up on her husband is scarier than staying in their defective marriage.

If you find yourself in a similar situation to Jane or any of the other people mentioned, this book is for you. If you believe that you are part of a co-dependent relationship, this book will guide you as you work towards overcoming co-dependency and eliminating controlling behavior while learning to feel fulfilled by your own life. This book can also help if you have a spouse, partner, or a friend who is co-dependent because you will learn to understand what drives their behavior, and how it can be modified. If you're ready to commit to the change that's required to turn the dynamics in your relationship around, then let's get started!

Chapter 1: What Exactly Is Co-Dependent Behavior?

Co-dependent behavior can be difficult to identify. Like a well-wrapped gift, it often comes in a pleasing wrapper in the form of false compassion. Compassion is an admirable value that many would like to develop but false compassion is not. It is exhausting and unhealthy. It turns you into a co-dependent individual who is caught in the illusion of helping others when, in reality, you are overlooking your own needs and feelings.

Do you feel like you or your loved one displays co-dependent behavior? If you are having trouble determining whether or not you are suffering from such a destructive behavior, here are a few co-dependent personalities that can help you recognize the traits.

The Saint

Putting the needs of others above your own is a very noble thing to do. In your relationship, you turn a blind eye on your partner's abusive behavior. Even if you are hurt emotionally and/or physically, you still choose to give. You still serve and care for the people who treat you poorly. You go down the path of martyrdom, neglecting your need to receive love and care. Paradoxically, the very things that you want are the reasons you give unconditionally but instead of being loved and cared for in return, you are taken for granted.

The Superhero

Life is full of troubles but thanks to you, your partner is saved from all his problems. If he is stuck in a financial rut, you quickly bail him out by offering financial aid. A while later, he comes up to you and relates another sad story about a bad investment. You feel sorry for him and it hurts your heart to see him suffering so you shell out more money to "help" him. Helping is good and once in a while, people that we love need our help. But you take helping to a whole new level. You feel so responsible for his comfort and well-being that you strip him off his ability to be self-reliant. You pamper and tolerate him thinking that what you are doing is right.

The Counselor

In your group of friends or in your family, you are the adviser. You love to give advice to other people— both solicited and unsolicited. You consider yourself as one of the few people who can see through a person. You feel like you can easily connect with somebody else thus you have an insight of what they truly feel. You rely so much on your "spider sense" that you forget to listen. Instead of helping other people, you are only making their problems worse. You are also feeding your insecurities. Constantly telling someone what to do with their lives shows that you are needy and insecure. Instead of showing strength, it shows weakness.

The Pleaser

You love doing things for your friends and family. You always volunteer during community events and you do not fail to help your neighbors when you feel they are in need. You don't mind buying coffee for the whole group at work, either. Because of what you do, people praise you and you feel loved. You bask in the attention and you convince yourself that you are surrounded by people who adore you. However, you feel disappointed when someone does not adequately appreciate your efforts. You start to question if you haven't been doing enough. Then you start to feel you are being taken for granted.

The "Yes" Man

You have perfected the art of saying "yes" to just about anything. You say "yes" to other people even if you truly mean to say "no." But because of your fears, you suppress your emotions and you just agree anyway. You think that this is a healthy habit because it helps you avoid conflict and argument, but you are doing damage to yourself. You are putting aside your own needs and feelings to make way for other people. You live your life with the fear to express your emotions. You basically live your life in hiding.

If you display one or more of the qualities described above, you have a co-dependent attitude and most likely, you and your partner are in a co-dependent relationship. This is not the end of the road for you. There is still a chance for you to work on your relationship to make it healthier for you both.

Chapter 2: Realizing Where It Stems from

Behavioral experts trace co-dependent behavior to having a traumatic childhood experience. Most of the co-dependent cases that they have handled present a history of having a childhood filled with addiction, neglect and abuse. They have observed that their patients have developed co-dependent behaviors for survival.

Through observation, one can see that people in co-dependent relationships manifest child-like behavior. An example of these is categorical thinking. People manifesting co-dependent behavior see situations in black and white, with no shades in between. This way of thinking leads them to over-react when faced with certain situations. Let's take Cathy's case for example. Cathy is an elementary school teacher and for the first time, her lecture was evaluated. During the evaluation, it was commented that her teaching skills need improvement. Instead of improving herself, Cathy chose to resign and apply to another school.

Another child-like behavior that co-dependent individuals possess is personalization. This habit involves interpreting everything that is said and done in their environment as if it were directed solely at them. This causes co-dependent persons to develop a paranoid perspective which results in hostile actions and behavior. Some even opt to isolate themselves socially. This behavior is evident in the case of Amy, a victim of abuse during her childhood. She was sexually molested by her father and because of what happened to her, she has grown to loathe the company of men. Since her childhood years, she has refused to open up to male classmates, co-workers and even relatives. She also decided not to marry. She grew up with the belief that she doesn't need a man but, in truth, she has trust issues.

Over-analyzing is also one of the typical child-like behaviors of a co-dependent individual. They tend to think too much and end up stressing themselves out due to excessive and unnecessary anxiety. When faced with a dilemma, their minds go round in circles until their emotional systems break down.

If you or your partner had a traumatic childhood experience, there are several ways that you can let go of it. With support and the proper mindset, you can change your disposition and be healed from your painful past.

Chapter 3: Recognizing Childhood Trauma

Experiencing trauma during your childhood can have a severe and lasting effect on your life. Even as a grown up, you still see the world as a frightening and dangerous place; the same way that you had seen it when you were young. When your trauma remains unresolved, it can lead to co-dependent relationships and ultimately an unhappy life. It will also lead you to further trauma and emotional abuse.

Childhood trauma results from anything that endangers a child's safety and security. This includes:

- An unsafe environment
- Separation from a parent/both parents
- Traumatic medical procedures
- Severe illness
- Sexual, physical, emotional or verbal abuse
- Domestic violence
- Bullying

People react to trauma in different ways but here are common symptoms that have manifested in individuals who have undergone childhood trauma:

- o Sudden mood swings
- o Irrational irritability and anger
- o Constant feelings of sadness or hopelessness
- o Self-blame and guilt
- o Confusion
- o Unnecessary anxiety
- o Social withdrawal
- o Insomnia
- o Bodily aches and pains
- o Fatigue
- o Muscle tension

There are also other symptoms that can be observed in a co-dependent individual, but there are some people who have learned to suppress these symptoms. Outwardly they seem to live quite a normal life. They maintain good friendships with other people and a stable career. However, a look into their relationships with their partners, will prove that there is truly something wrong. You will be able to see that they are living in a co-dependent relationship.

If you are experiencing the following symptoms and if you are in a co-dependent relationship, there are many ways that a psychiatrist or a trauma specialist can help you in your recovery. Here are a few common therapies that you might want to try.

Cognitive-Behavioral Therapy

This kind of therapy involves counseling with a medical professional. Although it doesn't treat the physiological effect of childhood trauma, it can help you develop a positive mindset that can help you overcome your childhood fears. It will involve opening up and talking about your past. It may sound scary and you might be hesitant to talk about it, but it is only through opening yourself up that your psychiatrist can understand what you went through. Sharing your experiences can also have a freeing effect. Some victims of childhood trauma kept silent for so many years, because they felt they couldn't trust others. This is normal but if you feel that way, you have to learn to trust your psychiatrist. Choose a psychiatrist with whom you are comfortable and can trust to guide you toward recovery. Let go of your doubts and for the first time in your life, be free of the weight you have been carrying for so long.

Somatic Experiencing

This method makes use of the body's ability to heal itself. Somatic Experiencing focuses on bodily sensation rather than on thoughts and memories about your traumatic experience. This is a good alternative if you are hesitant about expressing how you feel. With a meditation-like process, you concentrate on what's happening in your body and you gradually learn to get in touch with trauma-related energy. From there, your body's natural survival instincts take over and you will find yourself releasing all the negative energy pent up inside you. You will experience various forms of physical release such as screaming, crying and shaking.

EMDR (Eye Movement Desensitization and Reprocessing)

This is a relatively new method but many patients have reported positive results. EMDR incorporates elements of cognitive-behavioral therapy with eye movement stimulation, which is said to make it easier to unlock and resolve traumatic memories. After stimulating eye movement through simple exercises, you will undergo counseling with your chosen psychiatrist.

Hypnotherapy

Hypnotherapy is a popular form of treatment for people dealing with trauma. Many scientific studies claim the efficacy of hypnotherapy and a lot of patients who have used the method have also reported that they were able to recover quickly. The main goal of this treatment is to unlock suppressed emotions so that trauma can be explored from a different and healthier perspective. There are many forms of hypnotherapy and the advice of a competent practitioner can help in determining which one is right for you. A hypnotist will usually begin by performing an evaluation of your personal circumstances and from there, he will determine what approach to take. Generally, hypnotherapy practitioners use cognitive or analytical hypnotherapy which works on a deeper level compared to other types of hypnosis. Like a psychiatrist, a hypnotherapist will treat your problems with sensitivity and utmost understanding. He will guide you through your treatment plan and discuss it with you thoroughly before you begin treatment.

Chapter 4: Gaining New Perspectives

Meditation allows an individual to heal on a different level. By taking a spiritual perspective, meditating can help an individual explore new perspectives within himself and get to know himself better. It also promotes a heightened consciousness which allows better discipline over one's behavior. This is why many individuals turn to meditation as a solution for their co-dependent behavior. Some couples also engage themselves in meditation that involves them working together. Many people have reported positive results in using meditation to overcome co-dependent behavior and relationships, so you might also want to give this a try. If you meditate regularly, then this should a familiar procedure for you. On the other hand, if this is your first attempt at meditation, have no worries. Meditation is relatively easy to understand and to do, as long as you trust that it will yield results. Being open-minded is the main prerequisite for meditation, and if you are negative about trying this method, you will not feel its effects on your life. Be open and be healed.

There are many kinds of meditation that you can apply. If you are already a practitioner, you can come up with a personalized meditation that will work for you. However, if you are not familiar with meditation yet, here are several methods that you can try.

Inner Child Meditation

Each individual has an "inner child." This inner child is shaped according to experiences during our childhood years. Happy childhoods produce an inner child who is at peace while traumatic childhoods create a wounded one. A wounded inner child develops into a co-dependent adult who involves himself in an equally co-dependent relationship. If you want to break free of co-dependency and if you want to heal your co-dependent relationship, you can start within yourself by healing your inner child.

One of the best ways to heal your inner child is through writing. Start by keeping a daily journal where you can communicate with your inner child regularly. In writing to your inner child, you have to address it lovingly the same way that you would an actual child. Start by writing: "My precious Mary" or "My little Victor." Tell your inner child that you are sorry for everything that he went through in the past and assure him that his sufferings have now come to an end. You have to make your inner child trust the adult-you for protection and care. Be sure to express your love for your inner child. Do not hold back. Fill your inner child with as much love and care as you possibly can.

When you are finished, transfer the pen or pencil that you are using to your other hand. Allow your inner child to respond by writing freely through your other hand. Insights and feelings will rush into your mind as you write down ideas on behalf of your inner child.

At first, angry and hurt words will come out. This is normal for wounded inner children. Because of their traumatic experiences, they are bitter and angry. But as you continue to practice this meditation daily, your inner child will eventually soften. His words will change and you will feel that he is improving. The harsh words will turn into positive ones and the guilt will turn into joy.

There are also some forms of inner child meditation that you can do in between your busy schedule. If you are caught up with the demands of your job or household responsibilities, you can opt to try a walking meditation. This form of meditation will only take a few minutes of your time but it can significantly contribute to your inner child's healing.

Take some time off to take a walk in a relaxed environment, like a quiet park or by a river. If there is a quiet hallway in your office building, it can work too. Start your walking meditation by building a relaxed environment within yourself. Clear your mind off stress and daily responsibilities. Stop thinking about what you need to do after your meditation. Instead, focus only on one person—your inner child. Stabilize your breathing by taking in deep breaths through your nose and exhaling through your mouth.

As soon as you are relaxed, concentrate on bringing out all your affection. It helps to visualize it building inside you. Once you have drawn out all the love inside you, breathe in deeply and say these words, "My inner child has arrived." Then breathe out and continue by saying, "My inner child is home now, safe and loved." This is a very simple meditation but with constant practice, it can help your wounded inner child to open up and be healed.

Meditation to Promote Inner Change

If you had a happy childhood but are struggling with co-dependent behavior, you can still use meditation. Meditation has also been helpful to individuals who want to cultivate a change in themselves. Meditation to promote inner change is also simple to do and can be done in your home.

Find a relaxing and quiet environment where you can perform your meditation. It must be free from any form of distraction to make sure that your concentration is not broken. Once you have found a room conducive to meditation, you are ready to start the meditation process.

Seat yourself or lie down in a comfortable position. You have to be careful not to fall asleep. With your mind in a relaxed state, it is easy to doze off so sitting on a chair or cross-legged on the floor is recommended.

Next, relax your mind by letting go of your worries. Stop thinking about work and chores that you need to do. Concentrate only on yourself and being in the present. Listen to the silence that surrounds you and let it calm your mind. Relax your body by breathing properly. Take deep breaths, inhale through your nose and slowly exhale through your mouth.

When you feel relaxed, start to visualize the negative energy inside you. Imagine it as a red light. Gather it all together and release it. Let it flow out of you. Let the red light slowly disappear from within you as you start to feel free from negativity and your negative behaviors. Empty yourself to make room for the new. When the red light has disappeared, with all of your conviction, say these words: "I refuse to be co-dependent" or "I will love myself more." Feel the meaning of those words. Do not simply say them. Mean them.

Gradually return to your awareness and open your eyes. Keep practicing this meditation regularly until you are able to experience results. This meditation should open you up to changing yourself for the better. It should help you let go of your co-dependent behavior and welcome a healthier, happier you. Results do not happen in one night. It takes time for inner change to occur, so be patient. Just keep believing that your constant practice will produce results, and you will get them, in time.

Chapter 5: Understanding a Co-Dependent Partner

Living with a partner who is struggling with co-dependent behavior can be difficult. Too often, you find yourself in an emotionally challenging situation where you have to do everything that you can to understand the other person's behavior. If you have a spouse or a partner who exhibits co-dependent behavior, do not give up. This is not the end of your relationship. There is still so much that you can do to help the person towards recovery. Usually, people who display co-dependent behavior are not aware of their actions. Because they justify the way they act, they think that what they are doing is right. If you truly care for your spouse or your partner, then do your best to aide them along the path to recovery.

Be Patient and Understanding

These are two important characteristics that you need to develop if you want to help your partner. It will be difficult to deal with their behavior and often you will find yourself thinking of giving up. Be patient and be understanding. Try to understand their situation. If your partner has been through a traumatic childhood that resulted in co-dependent behavior, try to put yourself in the partner's shoes. It is not easy to deal with a painful past. Try to understand that what he or she is going through is nowhere near simple.

Communicate Effectively

Communicating with your co-dependent partner will be a difficult task, especially if he or she does not want to explore the past. People with a painful childhood tend to clam up even to their spouses, so it is important for you to learn how to communicate effectively. In dealing with co-dependent people, it also helps to be honest with them about their behavior. If you confront them about their behavior, do it in a gentle manner. Do not attack them by being too direct. Just let them know that you are there to offer them support, constantly reminding them that you love them, too. Do not condemn them, because they did not choose to grow into the people that they have become. Victims of trauma will be damaged further if you try to be hard on them, so be sure to be subtle with your words and demonstrate understanding.

Encourage Them to See a Therapist or Join a Support Group

Your co-dependent partner may be hesitant to see a therapist or join a support group that can help

34

him/her recover. This is normal. Your partner might either be in denial or he may have difficulties trusting other people so you must take measures to help the person feel at ease and find a therapist that he or she can trust. Do not choose by yourself and impose your choice. Instead, let the partner determine a therapist with whom he/she feels comfortable opening up to. There are also some support groups that can help your spouse or partner to overcome trauma. Opening up to other people, even to complete strangers, can be overwhelming so do not be forceful. Just do your research and let him/her know which support groups exist in your community, and allow the decision to join such a group be made over time without any undue pressure from you.

Do Not Take Their Behavior Personally

If your loved one is a victim of a traumatic childhood, there are instances in your relationship that he/she may become irritable. He/she may anger easily or become defensive without provocation. There will also be times when you will notice that he/she is withdrawn or seems emotionally distant. Do not blame yourself for his behavior. Always remember that your partner's behavior is a result of the trauma that he/she experienced. Instead of reacting negatively and making the situation worse for you both, try to be understanding. Do not take it personally.

Conclusion

Changing yourself can be a long process. Shaping your character is not as easy as whipping up a meal in the kitchen. It can take years and a lot of patience. As you work towards recovery, expect that you will go through struggles. The road to recovery is not a walk in the park. You will be making decisions that you don't like. You will also be facing certain issues that you have tried to run away from. Sometimes, it can even mean having to let go of some people who negatively influence your life. As painful and as long as the path to recovery might be, do not allow yourself to give up. Change is difficult but it is not impossible.

You still have a chance at having a happy and normal life. If you work on changing yourself, you can enjoy having a healthy relationship with a partner who positively influences your life. You can build friendships that are not toxic, too. There is so much to look forward to as you fight to overcome co-dependence.

If you truly care for your loved one, take the first step to recovery now. Break the chains of co-dependency in your relationship by starting with yourself. Think of all the good that awaits you and your loved one if you make the change. Do not wait for your partner to give up on you. As much as he/she loves you, someday the limit will be reached. Your partner should love him/herself, too. Do your relationship a favor. If you have children, do it for them too. Take charge of your life now. Start the change that your relationship needs.

Finally, I'd like to thank you for purchasing this book! If you found it helpful, I'd greatly appreciate it if you'd take a moment to leave a review on Amazon. Thank you!

Made in the USA
Middletown, DE
14 January 2022

58709859R00024